THE DARING MISS QUIMBY

by Suzanne George Whitaker
illustrated by Catherine Stock

Holiday House / New York

Library of Congress Cataloging-in-Publication Data
Whitaker, Suzanne.
The daring Miss Quimby / by Suzanne George Whitaker ; illustrated by Catherine Stock. — 1st ed.
p. cm.
ISBN 978-0-8234-1996-8 (hardcover)
1. Quimby, Harriet, 1875-1912—Juvenile literature.
2. Women air pilots—United States—Biography—Juvenile literature.
3. Air pilots—United States—Biography—Juvenile literature.
I. Stock, Catherine, Ill. II. Title.
TL540.Q496W49 2009
629.13092—dc22
[B]
2008022569

ACKNOWLEDGMENTS

Harriet Quimby's story is an inspiration, tragedy, and legend worth relating to future generations.
I am indebted to Brigadier General Ed Y. Hall, Ret., of Spartanburg, South Carolina, for opening up
his extensive collection of books and articles to me, and offering me a glimpse into Harriet's world.

The publisher would like to thank him for reviewing the book for historical accuracy.

The quote "Twasn't very fast . . ." is from Harriet Quimby's October 4, 1906, article
in *Leslie's Illustrated Weekly* (see Selected Bibliography).

Photograph used by permission from the files of the Holbrook Heritage Room,
located at Coldwater Public Library, Coldwater, Michigan.

Harriet Quimby Stamp © 1991 United States Postal Service.
All Rights Reserved. Used with Permission.

Dedicated to my loving family,
with deepest affection to Mom,
Grace, and Hope
—S. G. W.

For Jude
—C. S.

HARRIET QUIMBY was the picture of a modern American woman of 1912. She drove a sporty roadster, worked as a writer, and had her own apartment. Harriet was a smart woman who loved to laugh and spend time with her friends . . . but most of all, Harriet was daring.

In 1903, when Harriet was twenty-eight, she decided to move across the country, from her home in California to New York City. Harriet loved the hustle and bustle of city life and quickly settled into her new job as a magazine writer.

Harriet's sense of adventure soon showed itself in her writing. Once, when Harriet was covering a story about a race car, the driver decided to put Harriet to the test. As she held on tight to the top of her hat, the driver circled the track at nearly one hundred miles per hour. But Harriet didn't scare easily. After the ride was over, she simply retied the hat ribbon under her chin and said, "Twasn't very fast; can't you make one hundred and twenty?"

It was at an air show in October 1910 that Harriet decided what her next daring adventure would be: She would learn to fly.

Air shows were very popular in the early 1900s, because people got to see flying machines up close and meet their newest heroes: the pilots. The planes weren't at all like the jets of today. They looked more like bicycles with wings, and flying them was dangerous.

Harriet, however, had made up her mind. But friends and family thought she had gone too far this time. After all, racing around in a fast car was one thing, but flying up in the wild blue yonder was quite another. Harriet smiled and told them she was going to try it anyway.

After three months and thirty-three lessons, Harriet was ready for her licensure test. On July 31, 1911, Harriet made her attempt. She was required by the Aero Club to complete five figure eights in the air, plus land the plane within 100 feet of a painted spot on the ground. Harriet failed on her first try, coming up 40 feet short of the 100-foot perimeter. Steadfast in her determination to succeed, Harriet tried the test again the very next day.

This time she succeeded. Early on the morning of August 1, 1911, Harriet became the first woman in the United States to earn a pilot's license, missing the painted spot on the ground by only 7 feet. A crowd had gathered to watch, and they all cheered as Harriet climbed out of her airplane. Harriet was issued pilot's license number 37 and made history.

People around the country heard about Harriet and her daring deed. They clamored to read stories about her or to catch a glimpse of her at a local air show. The whole country was just wild about Harriet. They couldn't get enough.

Harriet loved the attention and liked being different from the other pilots. To be sure that her fans could see her among the others in the air, Harriet designed her own special flight suit. It was purple and made of shiny satin. It had a hood; gloves; and tall, leather, lace-up boots. Harriet's flight suit made her stand out, and her fans loved it.

In 1912 the daring Miss Quimby took on her next adventure. She decided to be the first woman to fly across the English Channel, which is a big body of water running between England and France.

Crossing the English Channel in 1912 was considered very dangerous, and only the best pilots even thought about trying it. Harriet practiced her flying every day; and finally, when she felt ready, she packed her purple flight suit and took a boat to England.

On Tuesday, April 16, 1912, at 3:30 a.m., Harriet decided the time had come to make her next daring idea a reality. By 5:30 a.m. she had put on her purple suit, an overcoat, and a pair of wool gloves; stuck a hot-water bottle in her jacket; and climbed into the cockpit. She gave a thumbs-up to her mechanic, who gave the wooden propeller a hard swing; and the engine sprang to life. Puffs of smoke from the exhaust of the plane floated over the six men holding onto the machine. They let go, and Harriet was flying.

Harriet was scared. The fog was too thick to see through, and the temperature was very cold. She could not see anything around her and could only rely on her compass for direction. Finally, at 7:00 a.m., the fog partially cleared and Harriet saw the white beaches of France.

She landed the plane on the shore near a fishing village called Hardelot. Harriet was so excited that she jumped from the cockpit to the soft sand below. A crowd of fishermen, women, and children ran to greet her. They lifted Harriet on their shoulders and even prepared a celebration breakfast for her, right there on the beach! Harriet Quimby had once again made history. She was the first woman to fly, by herself, across the English Channel.

Good news traveled fast in 1912, and Harriet hoped word of her daring flight would be splashed across the front page of every paper. What Harriet didn't know was that the world had turned its eyes to another news story—this one of tragedy, not triumph. The ship named the *Titanic* had sunk.

At first it seemed as if no one had noticed Harriet's flight, but that wasn't true. People who loved airplanes and pilots had noticed, and soon Harriet was once again the talk of the town. Fans of Harriet flocked to air shows and sometimes waited hours to get an autograph or have a picture taken with the purple-hooded flyer.

Harriet performed in shows all over the country, but it was at an air show in Boston, on July 1, 1912, that Harriet made her last flight. Showing off her new, two-seater plane from France, Harriet agreed to take William Willard, manager of the Boston air show, for a test flight. They were at an altitude of 1,000 feet, getting ready to land, when the plane suddenly tilted forward. The move flung Mr. Willard out of his seat, and he plunged to his death in Boston Harbor.

Onlookers said that although Harriet temporarily gained control over the spinning plane, she lost it again. A few moments later, Harriet was thrown out of the pilot's seat and fell to her death in the harbor as well.

Only eleven months after first beginning to fly, thirty-seven-year-old Harriet Quimby had died.

But Harriet's love of adventure and her pioneering spirit lived on. She envisioned the day it would be possible for women to soar through the skies and have a career in flying if they desired one. In part because of her efforts, female pilots such as Amelia Earhart, Bessie Coleman, Anne Lindbergh, and even astronaut Sally Ride could now fulfill *their* daring dreams.

WOMEN IN AVIATION TIME LINE

1906 – E. Lillian Todd is the first woman to design and build an aircraft.

1908 – Madame Thérèse Peltier is the first woman to fly an airplane solo.

1910 – Baroness Raymonde de Laroche obtains a license from the Aéro Club de France. She is the first woman in the world to earn her pilot's license.

1911 – August 1 – Harriet Quimby becomes the first woman in America, and the second in the world, to receive her pilot's license.

1911 – September 4 – Harriet Quimby becomes the first woman to fly at night.

1912 – April 16 – Harriet Quimby becomes the first woman to pilot her own aircraft across the English Channel.

1916 – Ruth Law sets two American records flying from Chicago to New York.

1921 – Bessie Coleman becomes the first African American, male or female, to earn a pilot's license.

1928 – June 17 – Amelia Earhart is the first woman to fly across the Atlantic Ocean.

1929 – Amelia Earhart becomes the first president of the Ninety-Nines, an organization of women pilots.

1930 – Anne Morrow Lindbergh becomes the first woman to earn a glider pilot's license.

1932 – May 20–21 – Amelia Earhart is the first woman to fly solo across the Atlantic Ocean.

1937 – Amelia Earhart is lost over the Pacific Ocean.

1953 – Jacqueline Cochran becomes the first woman to break the sound barrier.

1983 – Dr. Sally Ride becomes the first American woman in space on the shuttle *Challenger*.

1994 – April 21 – Jackie Parker becomes the first woman to qualify to fly an F-16 combat plane.

1999 – Lt. Col. Eileen Collins (USAF) is the first female space shuttle commander.

AUTHOR'S NOTE

HARRIET QUIMBY was a daring woman for 1912, and some would say a daring woman no matter what the year. She fought hard for what she wanted and had the courage to turn her dreams into reality.

Harriet was born into humble beginnings, a fact that she would later try to hide from the public. Her father, a Civil War veteran and an unsuccessful farmer, uprooted the family from their rural Michigan home and transplanted them to California.

According to the 1900 San Francisco census, Harriet listed her occupation as "actress." Although with her charm and stellar good looks, this career was a logical choice for a woman of that era, Harriet had more success with her career in writing.

Harriet began writing occasional articles for the *San Francisco Dramatic Review*, the *San Francisco Chronicle*, and the *San Francisco Call*. Soon she won the respect of the all-male editorial staff at the *Chronicle*, which offered her a permanent byline. Eventually Harriet had the opportunity to combine her love of the theater with her writing skill. She joined forces with her friend D. W. Griffith, adapting several scripts into films, which made Harriet one of the first female screenwriters.

In 1903 Harriet joined the staff of *Leslie's Illustrated Weekly* in New York City. At first her articles focused on home and household tips, but quickly Harriet's adventurous spirit began to leak through. She wrote about how women could find jobs and safe apartments, budget income, and repair cars.

An assignment pulled her into the world of air shows, and in 1910 she saw her first. The air meets of 1910 were perhaps some of the most famous of their day. Big names such as Claude Grahame-White from England, Alfred Leblanc from France, and Americans Ralph Johnstone and Arch Hoxsey, who flew for Orville and Wilbur Wright, were all there. All these dashing and daring pilots were considered celebrities and flying heroes. To ramp up the action at the shows,

pilots competed for prize money. Awards ranged anywhere from $500 to $45,000 to entice the best pilots to attend and compete in the shows.

All the fame and fortune came at a high price. Most pilots survived only a few years, many dying while performing the very stunts for which they had been so handsomely rewarded weeks earlier.

When Harriet died, people who admired her and loved flying decided that the time had come to make some changes in flight safety. First, they added seat belts to the pilot and passenger seats. Next, Harriet's friend Leo Stevens developed a reliable parachute and harness for pilots to wear while they were flying. Finally, airplane builders made planes bigger, and covered more of the machines with metal, so that pilots and passengers might have a chance to survive a crash.

For a long time Harriet's legacy faded into the shadows as other female aviators took their turns in the spotlight.

Then, seventy-nine years later, people started talking about Harriet Quimby again. In April 1991 the United States Postal Service issued a special stamp of Harriet, complete with her picture on it in her famous purple flight suit. In July 2004, a whopping ninety-two years after her plane crashed, Harriet was inducted into the National Aviation Hall of Fame.

SUGGESTED WEBSITES

About Harriet:

www.pbs.org/kcet/chasingthesun/innovators/hquimby.html

www.pbs.org/wgbh/nova/bleriot/quimby.html

Women and Aviation:

The Ninety-Nines: International Organization of Women Pilots: www.ninety-nines.org

Smithsonian National Air and Space Museum: www.nasm.si.edu

WASP, women pilots of World War II: www.wasp-wwii.org

SELECTED BIBLIOGRAPHY

Hall, Ed. *Harriet Quimby: America's First Lady of the Air.* Spartanburg, SC: Honoribus Press, 1990.

Holden, Henry M. *Her Mentor was an Albatross: The Autobiography of Pioneer Pilot Harriet Quimby.* Mt. Freedom, NJ: Blackhawk Publishing, 1993.

London Daily Mirror, "American Woman First to Cross Channel," April 17, 1912.

Phipps, Walter H. "The Danger of Lifting Tail and its Probable Bearing on the Death of Miss Quimby." *Aircraft,* August 1912.

Quimby, Harriet. "A Woman's Exciting Ride in a Racing Motor Car." *Leslie's Illustrated Weekly,* October 4, 1906.

———. "How I Won My Aviator's License." *Leslie's Illustrated Weekly,* August 24, 1911.

———. "We Girls Who Fly and What We're Afraid of." *Leslie's Illustrated Weekly,* February 2, 1912.